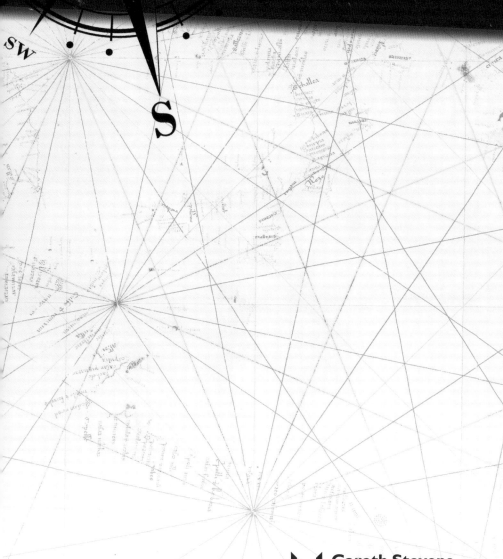

UNDERSTANDING MAPS OF OUR WORLD

MAPS and NAVIGATION

Gareth Stevens
Publishing

Please visit our Web site www.garethstevens.com. For a free color catalog of all our high-quality books, call toll free 1-800-542-2595 or fax 1-877-542-2596.

Library of Congress Cataloging-in-Publication Data
Maps and navigation / Tim Cooke, editor.
      p. cm. -- (Understanding maps of our world)
   Includes index.
   ISBN 978-1-4339-3509-1 (library binding) -- ISBN 978-1-4339-3510-7 (pbk.)
   ISBN 978-1-4339-3511-4 (6-pack)
   1. Nautical charts. I. Cooke, Tim.
 GA359.M36 2010
 623.89--dc22   2009039213

Published in 2010 by
Gareth Stevens Publishing
111 East 14th Street, Suite 349
New York, NY 10003

© 2010 The Brown Reference Group Ltd.

For Gareth Stevens Publishing:
Art Direction: Haley Harasymiw
Editorial Direction: Kerri O'Donnell

For The Brown Reference Group Ltd:
Editorial Director: Lindsey Lowe
Managing Editor: Tim Cooke
Children's Publisher: Anne O'Daly
Design Manager: David Poole
Designer: Simon Morse
Production Director: Alastair Gourlay
Picture Manager: Sophie Mortimer
Picture Researcher: Clare Newman

Picture Credits:
Front Cover: Library of Congress; Shutterstock: Jim Barber br

Brown Reference Group: all artwork

Corbis: Agnese Battista 21; Bettmann 38; Commander John Leenhouts 39; DigitalVision: 4m, 4b, 42; iStock: Jodie Coston 11; Nathan Marx 8l; Mlenny 29; Jupiter Images: Ablestock 5m; Photos.com 18, 24; Stockxpert 5t, 28; Science Photo Library: 22; Shutterstock: 34; Kent Akgungor 14l; Auter 36; Steve Estvanik 31; Jose Galveia 40; Vladislav Gurfinkel 4t; Holger W. 16; Megastocker 44; Aleksandar Milosovic 41; Moschen 7; Steven Wright 5b

Publisher's note to educators and parents: Our editors have carefully reviewed the Web sites that appear on p. 46 to ensure that they are suitable for students. Many Web sites change frequently, however, and we cannot guarantee that a site's future contents will continue to meet our high standards of quality and educational value. Be advised that students should be closely supervised whenever they access the Internet.

Manufactured in the United States of America
1 2 3 4 5 6 7 8 9   12 11 10

CPSIA compliance information: Batch #BRW0102GS: For further information contact Gareth Stevens, New York, New York at 1-800-542-2595.

Contents

The Changing Shape of the World

This map shows the world known to Europeans in the fifteenth century: Europe and parts of Asia and Africa.

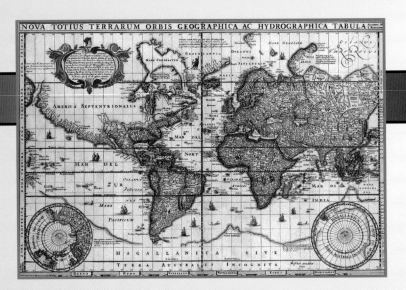

NOVA TOTIUS TERRARUM ORBIS GEOGRAPHICA AC HYDROGRAPHICA TABULA

In this seventeenth-century map, only the interior of North America and the southern oceans remain empty.

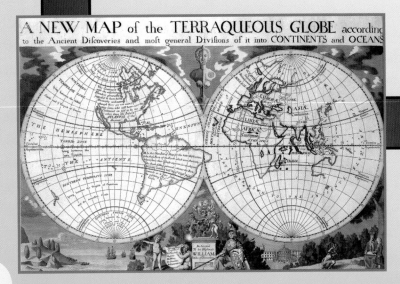

A NEW MAP of the TERRAQUEOUS GLOBE according to the Ancient Discoveries and most general Divisions of it into CONTINENTS and OCEANS

This map reveals more information about Australia, but the northwest coast of North America and most of the Pacific Ocean remain unknown.

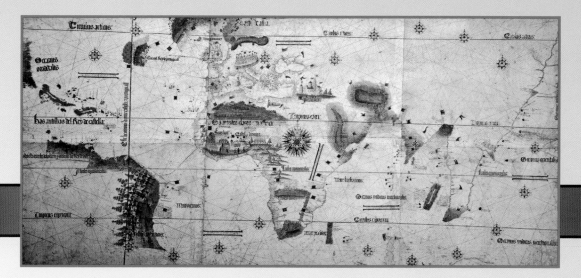

This sixteenth-century map fills in the coasts of Africa and India, the Caribbean islands, and parts of South America.

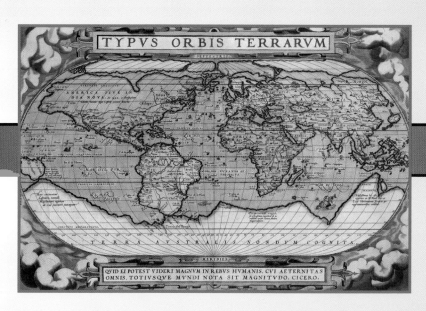

In this sixteenth-century map, South America is only roughly shaped; the northwest coast of Australia has become part of the legendary "southern continent."

The first photographs of Earth from space were taken in the 1960s.

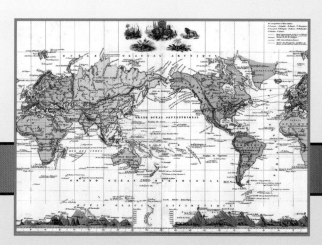

This world map was drawn in 1875, when Europeans were at the height of claiming colonies in other lands.

Introduction

This is a volume from the set Understanding Maps of Our World. This book looks at how maps and mapping help travelers find their way.

UNDERSTANDING MAPS OF OUR WORLD IS AN eight-volume set that describes the history of cartography, discusses its importance in different cultures, and explains how it is done. Cartography is the technique of compiling information for, and then drawing, maps or charts. Each volume in the set examines a particular aspect of mapping and uses numerous artworks and photographs to help the reader understand the sometimes complex themes.

After all, cartography is both a science and an art. It has existed since before words were written down and today uses the most up-to-date computer technology and imaging systems. Advances in mapmaking through history have been closely involved with wider advances in science and technology. Studying maps demands some understanding of math and at the same time an appreciation of visual creativity. Such a subject is bound to get a little complex at times!

About This Book

This book shows how navigational equipment and techniques have developed since the earliest travelers. Many brave explorers in the past literally "sailed into the unknown." Some did not even have a compass to help guide them. Today, long-distance travel in ships or airplanes requires complicated modern technology. There are many navigational aids, including the satellite equipment that forms the global positioning system (GPS). It can help pinpoint the traveler's position and figure out the best route to follow to ensure safe arrival.

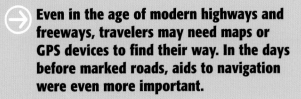
Even in the age of modern highways and freeways, travelers may need maps or GPS devices to find their way. In the days before marked roads, aids to navigation were even more important.

Using the Stars

Sailors have used navigation by the stars, or celestial navigation, for centuries to help them cross the world's seas and oceans.

FOR THOUSANDS OF YEARS, NAVIGATORS IN THE NORTHERN Hemisphere have relied on the Pole Star. This star is directly overhead at the North Pole. It seems to remain stationary while the other stars move around the night sky. That makes the Pole Star a reliable indicator of the direction of north. The Pole Star has had many names over time. Today it is known as Polaris. It is part of a pattern of stars, or constellation, known as Ursa Minor or the Little Dipper.

An easy way to locate Polaris is to find the constellation Ursa Major, or the Big Dipper. If you draw an imaginary line between the two stars on the side without the "handle," it points to Polaris.

In this time-lapse photograph of the night sky, the Pole Star appears as a bluish point in the center of a swirl of stars. The Pole Star was so important to navigators that it was once known as the Ship Star or the Steering Star.

Astronomers imagined that the stars were fixed to the inside of a celestial globe that surrounded Earth like a giant ball. That helped them identify star patterns. In fact, there is no celestial globe: Stars are either closer to or farther away from Earth.

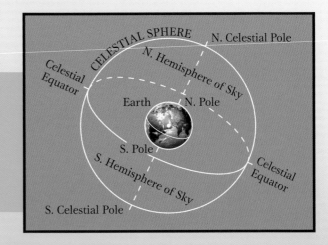

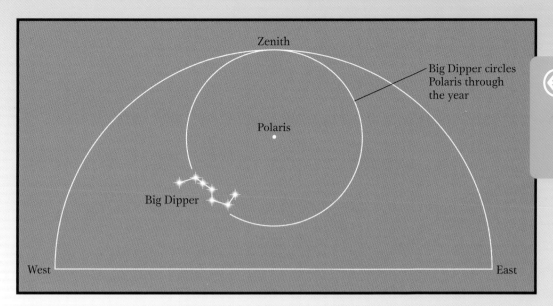

Zenith

Big Dipper circles Polaris through the year

Polaris

Big Dipper

West

East

Polaris can be found by following the two right-hand stars of the Big Dipper (the Pointers).

The Pole Star is not visible in the Southern Hemisphere. The night sky there is completely different. The closest equivalent to the Pole Star is a group of four stars called the Southern Cross. This small constellation is not strictly a cross because it is actually made up of five stars. An imaginary line through the long axis of the Southern Cross points to the south.

Using Star Patterns

Many centuries ago, sailors noticed that stars were not fixed in the night sky. Over time, the stars seemed to move across the sky, rising and setting at different points on the horizon. Navigators also realized that the points at which the stars rose and set at any one moment varied according to the observer's position. This knowledge could be used to help figure out where the observer was located on Earth. The more a navigator knew about the positions of different stars at different times, the better estimate he could make of his position. Early sailors sometimes gave names to the patterns of stars to help remember them. They also recorded the positions of the stars on maps. The Arabs, Persians, Micronesians, Polynesians, and inhabitants of the Indian Ocean islands all used detailed star maps to help them sail across the open oceans.

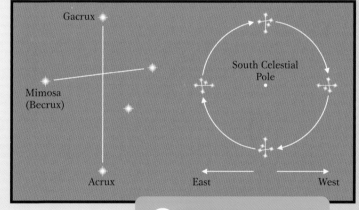

Gacrux

Mimosa (Becrux)

South Celestial Pole

Acrux

East

West

The direction of south is shown by the Southern Cross, a pattern of four bright stars in the sky of the Southern Hemisphere. A fifth star helps locate the cross. The cross circles the South Celestial Pole through the year, but it never dips below the horizon.

Early Navigation

Navigation became easier when voyagers were able to find the direction of north and south without looking at the stars. The vital discovery was the lodestone.

LODESTONE IS A HARD BLACK ROCK THAT HAS magnetic properties. In the twelfth century, Europeans discovered that, if they hung an oblong piece of the rock on a string, it would turn to align itself north to south. They called this a leading stone, or "lodestone." Lodestones were used to make magnetic compasses. By using a compass, ships could sail in the direction of their destination without needing to see land or the stars. However, the compass only told navigators in what direction they were heading, not how far they had traveled.

Early Navigation Instruments

The Pole Star not only indicated the direction of north; it had other useful qualities. Although it did not move across the skies like other stars, it did seem to

The cross-staff was a long stick with a shorter stick set at 90° that could slide along it. The sailor pointed the longer stick at a point midway between the horizon and a star. He then moved the crosspiece until the sight at one end was in line with the horizon and the sight at the other end was in line with the star. The farther away from the observer the shorter stick or transarm was along the staff, the farther south the observer was.

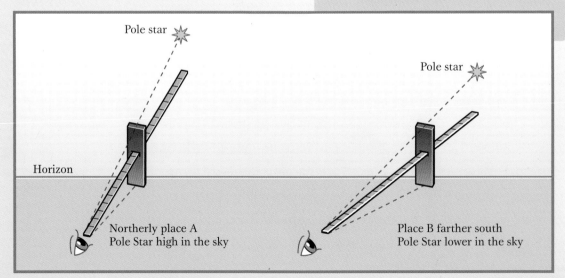

Horizon

Northerly place A
Pole Star high in the sky

Place B farther south
Pole Star lower in the sky

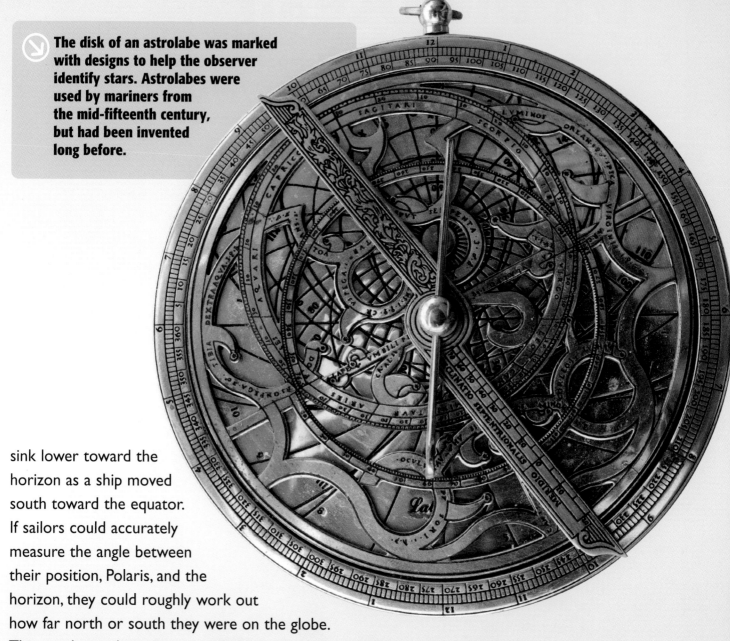

The disk of an astrolabe was marked with designs to help the observer identify stars. Astrolabes were used by mariners from the mid-fifteenth century, but had been invented long before.

sink lower toward the horizon as a ship moved south toward the equator. If sailors could accurately measure the angle between their position, Polaris, and the horizon, they could roughly work out how far north or south they were on the globe. This north–south position is called latitude. Various methods of measuring angles were developed for north–south positioning. Early navigators used the cross-staff (see diagram at left) and the astrolabe. The Greeks developed these two instruments to measure the altitude of the stars, sun, and moon.

The astrolabe was a disk of brass or iron with a pointer called an *alidade* pivoted at its center. One person hung the astrolabe from a string while another knelt down. This observer pointed the *alidade* at the sun or a star and read the angle from markings on the astrolabe. Astrolabes had lines on them that showed the relative positions of the constellations.

On the Ocean

As sailors traveled farther and farther across the world's oceans, they developed a number of different methods of finding their way.

PORTUGUESE SAILORS BUILT HUGE NAVIGATIONAL BEACONS on shore. These *padroes* were towers that were easily visible from the sea. Because they were each located at an exact latitude, they showed ship's pilots and navigators their precise north–south position.

But ships do not just sail north and south. Sailors needed a way of measuring how far they had traveled in whatever direction. The solution was the ship's log. The early form of log was simply a piece of wood attached to a long rope. The rope had equally spaced knots tied in it: there was usually a knot every 42 feet (12.8 m). When a reading was taken, the log was dropped overboard. It drifted behind the moving ship, pulling the rope off the deck. The sailors counted the number of knots pulled off the coiled rope over a set number of minutes. That enabled them to use simple math to calculate the speed of the ship. Once they knew their speed, they could calculate roughly how far they had traveled over a period of time.

The nautical measurement of speed, or knot, takes its name from this way of measuring distance. A knot represents 1 nautical mile per hour (1 nautical mile = 2,000 yards, not 1,760 yards, as in a standard mile).

> ⊙→ **The sextant is used to measure the angle of the sun above the horizon. The observer lines up the light rays from the horizon with those that come from the sun or a star, via a mirror.**

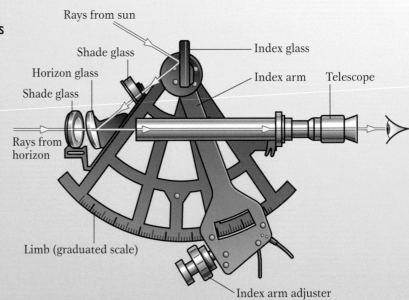

Rays from sun

Shade glass

Index glass

Horizon glass

Index arm   Telescope

Shade glass

Rays from horizon

Limb (graduated scale)

Index arm adjuster

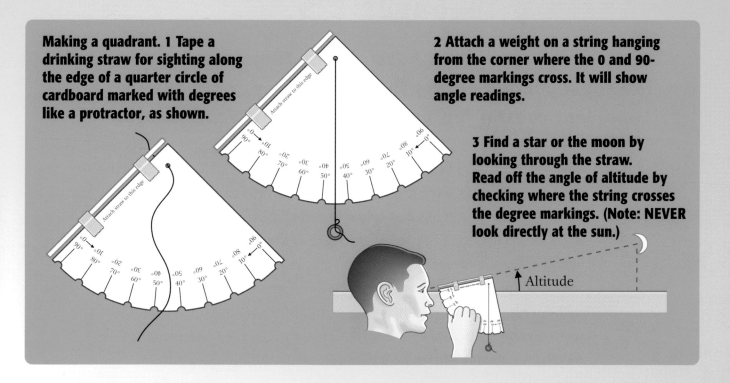

Making a quadrant. 1 Tape a drinking straw for sighting along the edge of a quarter circle of cardboard marked with degrees like a protractor, as shown.

2 Attach a weight on a string hanging from the corner where the 0 and 90-degree markings cross. It will show angle readings.

3 Find a star or the moon by looking through the straw. Read off the angle of altitude by checking where the string crosses the degree markings. (Note: NEVER look directly at the sun.)

Altitude

Improvements in Navigation Instruments

The quadrant was another important early instrument. It is a metal plate shaped like a quarter-circle. A weight hangs from the point where the two straight edges meet. The navigator sights the Pole Star or another celestial body along one edge of the quadrant, and the weighted string shows the star's angle above the horizon on the third, curved edge. The quadrant was very accurate—as long as it was possible to see the stars.

Like the quadrant, the sextant was used to measure the altitude of stars above the horizon. It used mirrors to bring together rays of light received from the horizon and from a star. The observer could then measure the angle between the two objects.

Having located a suitable star, the sailor consulted a nautical almanac. This was a book containing tables of figures that provided the positions of the stars, planets, sun, and moon at particular times of the day. If he knew the time, a navigator could use the almanac to establish his position. But although sailors could now measure their latitude accurately, it would be many years before it was possible to achieve the same accuracy about their position in an east–west direction, or longitude (see pages 22–23).

Early Charts

Early seafarers did not have charts. They traveled near the coast, mainly during the day, so they could see important coastal features. At night they went ashore.

AMONG THE MOST NOTABLE TRADERS AND SAILORS OF THE ancient world were the Phoenicians, who lived at the eastern end of the Mediterranean in what is now Israel and Lebanon from about 1100 B.C. to 600 B.C. They sailed throughout the Mediterranean and into the Atlantic Ocean, founding colonies in North Africa, Cyprus, and southern Spain. In the same way, the Indian Ocean was later dominated by Arab traders. They used the regular monsoon winds to sail back and forth across the ocean. By the eighth century A.D., they had set up merchant colonies all around its shores.

Arab sea pilots collected a vast store of navigational knowledge that was passed on from generation to generation. It was often written down on charts. These pilots found their way by using coastal landmarks or by measuring the

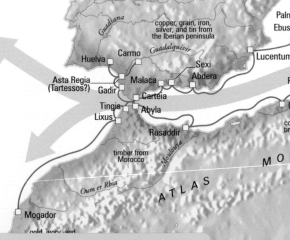

⬆ ➡ **Some ships that sail in the eastern Mediterranean today are still influenced by the ancient vesseis of the Phoenicians. The map shows how the Phoenicians established colonies throughout the Mediterranean and even in the Atlantic Ocean.**

depth and current of the water. They calculated the altitude of stars above the horizon by measuring finger widths above the horizon. These pilots were often hired by different ships or traders, so they guarded their charts to make sure that they would be hired again. Arabs refined the astrolabe from a primitive Greek instrument into a useful tool. They also used the compass and quadrant.

Although they did not have magnetic compasses or charts, the Vikings of Scandinavian were important traders. They were also fearsome raiders who attacked coastal settlements in northern Europe. When they sailed out of sight of land, Viking navigators looked for the Pole Star. In the far north, it never gets dark in the summer; sailors used the sun's position to navigate. Sometimes they released ravens. The birds would fly toward land if it was close enough (if not, they flew back to the ship). The sailors would follow birds that flew over the horizon.

Black Sea

Corsica

grain and silver from Sardinia

Praeneste △

APPENNINES

ALPS

BALKAN MTS

KÜRE MTS

Mago

Tharros

Sardinia

Kizil Irmak

Caralis

Sulcis

Nora

Panormos

Soluntum

Motya

Sicily

Lefkandi △

Zincirli △

Hippo Diarrhytus

Cossyra

Kerkouane

Olympia △

TAURUS MTS

Lake Tuz

Hippo Regius

Utica

Carthage

Hadrumetum

Thapsos

Leptis Minor

Acholla

Usilla

Malta

Tas Silg

Rhodes

Kommos ■

Crete

Salamis

Amathus

Idalion

Paphos

Cyprus

Kition

Sidon

Ugarit

Arvad

Byblos

Berytus

Tyre

Sarepta

Akhziv

'Atlit

Mediterranean Sea

dyes, grain, and olive oil from Tunisia

Girba

Oea

Sabrata

Leptis Magna

gold, ivory, and slaves from tropical Africa

Jerusalem

Gaza

dye, glass, metalwork, and textiles from Phoenicia

gold and slaves from tropical Africa

Sinai Peninsula

Nile

Red Sea

■ Canaanite Bronze Age city, from 2nd millennium BCE

■ Phoenician colony or trading post established in the 11th–9th centuries BCE

□ Phoenician colony or trading post established in the 8th–6th centuries BCE

△ other site with Phoenician finds

Phoenician expansion, 11th–6th centuries BCE

Phoenician heartland

coast under Phoenician influence by the 6th...

coast under Greek influence by the 6th ce...

Phoenician trade route

| 0 | | 600 km |
| 0 | | 400 mi |

15

Legendary Voyages

Christopher Columbus and Ferdinand Magellan changed the world map. Columbus discovered America and Magellan sailed all the way around the world.

EUROPEANS SAW EAST ASIA AS THE SOURCE OF VALUABLE trade goods, such as silks and spices. However, the overland trade routes across Asia were controlled by Muslim empires. The Italian mariner Christopher Columbus was convinced that he could reach east Asia by sailing west. Europeans at that time were not aware of North or South America or of the vast Pacific Ocean. For over 10 years, Columbus tried to raise money to pay for an expedition to explore trade routes to the west. Eventually, King Ferdinand and Queen Isabella of Spain gave him funds; in return, Columbus promised to bring back riches from east Asia, including gold, spices, and silk. Three ships, the *Nina*, *Pinta*, and *Santa Maria*, set sail on August 3, 1492, from Palos in Spain.

As an educated man, Columbus knew that Earth was not flat; but most of his crew were sure that it was. They also believed that there were places where the sea boiled or was full of monsters. As they sailed farther west, the crew became more and more worried. Columbus needed all of his skill as a leader to keep them under control. It must have been a relief when they sighted land in what is

Columbus's flagship *Santa Maria* was a type of cargo ship known as a carrack or nao. It was slow compared to his other two ships, which were caravels, but handled well in the Atlantic Ocean.

PO
P
H
Sc

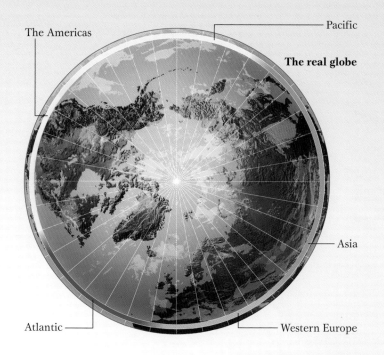

The Americas

Pacific

The real globe

Asia

Atlantic

Western Europe

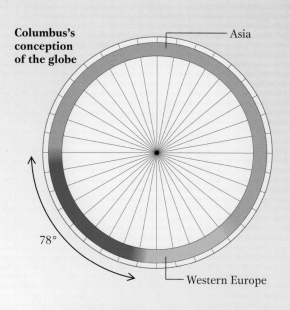

Columbus's conception of the globe

Asia

78°

Western Europe

Columbus's view of the world (above) was a huge miscalculation. Asia is far too big. The whole world is too small. The Pacific and the New World are unknown.

now the Bahamas. Believing that he had reached the "Indies" (Southeast Asia), Columbus called the people he met Indians. He eventually returned to Spain on March 15, 1493.

Columbus's achievements as a navigator were remarkable. He had only simple instruments, including a compass and a log. Covering about 150 miles a day, he worked out his position using a method called dead reckoning.

Discovering America Was a Mistake!

Even on his fourth voyage west, 10 years later, Columbus still believed that he was close to east Asia. There were two main reasons for his error. The first is that his calculation of distances was wrong. Columbus had studied a map of the world drawn by the ancient Greek geographer Ptolemy over 1,300 years earlier. But Ptolemy had made Asia seem much bigger than it really was. On the map, it wrapped around the world and so seemed much closer to the coast of western Europe than it really is. Second, Columbus underestimated the circumference of Earth by about one-quarter of the total distance. There was a third reason, too: Columbus believed he was in Asia because he wanted to believe it. Ferdinand and Isabella had invested their money because they wanted to control the east Asian trade routes and profit by bringing spices and silks home to Spain by sea.

Ferdinand Magellan

Portuguese-born Ferdinand Magellan was the first European to cross the Pacific Ocean. He was also the first person to circumnavigate, or sail all the way around, the world.

Like Columbus, Magellan wanted to discover new trade routes. His destination was the Moluccas in eastern Indonesia, which were also known as the Spice Islands. In 1517, Magellan offered his services to the king of Spain, and in 1519 he set off from Seville.

Magellan sailed across the Atlantic Ocean, where a ship wrecked and he had to stop a mutiny among his men. At the southern tip of South America, he sailed into the passage leading to the Pacific Ocean. This passage is today called the Strait of Magellan. After nearly 40 days, Magellan reached a huge ocean that he named the Pacific because it was peaceful and calm. Magellan reached the Marianas, or Ladrone Islands, on March 6, 1521. On March 16, he discovered the Philippines. Five weeks later, he was killed in a fight between local tribes. After Magellan's death, one of his ships continued west. The *Victoria* sailed around the Cape of Good Hope at the southern tip of Africa and then sailed north to reach Seville in 1522. The *Victoria* brought back a cargo of spices from the Moluccas that easily paid for the whole expedition.

Mapmakers Divide Up the World

Why did the Portuguese Magellan get support for his voyage from Spain? The answer lay in an agreement made in 1494 between the two great seagoing nations of Spain and Portugal. The Treaty of Tordesillas divided the world in two. Portugal would control trading routes and all lands east of a north–south line drawn "370 leagues west of the Cape Verde Islands" (see map, right). Spain would control everything west of the line. By studying maps, Magellan had decided that the Molucca Islands lay in Spain's half of the globe—which is why the Spanish monarch was eager to sponsor his voyage.

All trade areas to the left of the line belonged to Spain, all
to the right to Portugal. But no cartographer could extend
the line into a circle to cover the other side of the world.

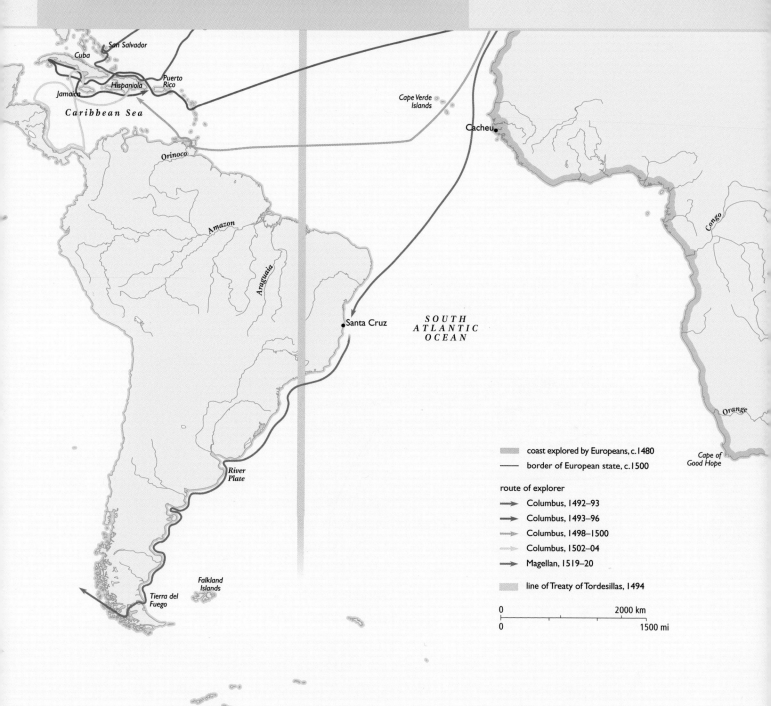

coast explored by Europeans, c.1480
border of European state, c.1500

route of explorer

Columbus, 1492–93
Columbus, 1493–96
Columbus, 1498–1500
Columbus, 1502–04
Magellan, 1519–20

line of Treaty of Tordesillas, 1494

0   2000 km
0   1500 mi

Portolan Charts

One of the earliest forms of coastal chart that we might recognize today as a map was the portolano, or portolan chart. Modern sea charts have many of the same features.

THE FIRST PORTOLANS APPEARED IN THE FOURTEENTH century in Italy. At first they were just written lists of directions for sailors. They did not contain any maps or illustrations. It was only later that they became actual charts.

At the same time portolan charts first appeared, Europeans were starting to use the compass (the Chinese had used compasses for hundreds of years). The charts often showed a web of criss-crossing lines, called rhumb lines, that helped in direction finding. These lines radiated out from the middle of wind roses—diagrams that showed the direction of prevailing winds. In the Mediterranean, the wind direction is very predictable. Wind roses showed main winds in black or gold lines and half winds in green lines. Often, though, wind roses were really just compass roses. They indicated directions rather than winds. Mapmakers in Catalonia (northeast Spain) and in Genoa and Venice (in Italy) produced the earliest portolan charts.

Portolans usually had the coastline marked, with place-names added. They also had scales of distance, a compass rose, and indications of hazards like islands, reefs, and currents. A port marked in red usually meant a safe haven. Portolans allowed sailors to plan their voyage and then follow its progress.

A Collection of Knowledge over Time

The chartmakers who created the early portolans achieved a high degree of accuracy. Sailors had built up knowledge of the Mediterranean over many centuries of seafaring. Contemporary mariners and traders were very familiar with distances and bearings between all the main ports and safe anchorages.

Beyond the locations of coastal features and the shape of the coastline, portolans provided very little information about anything

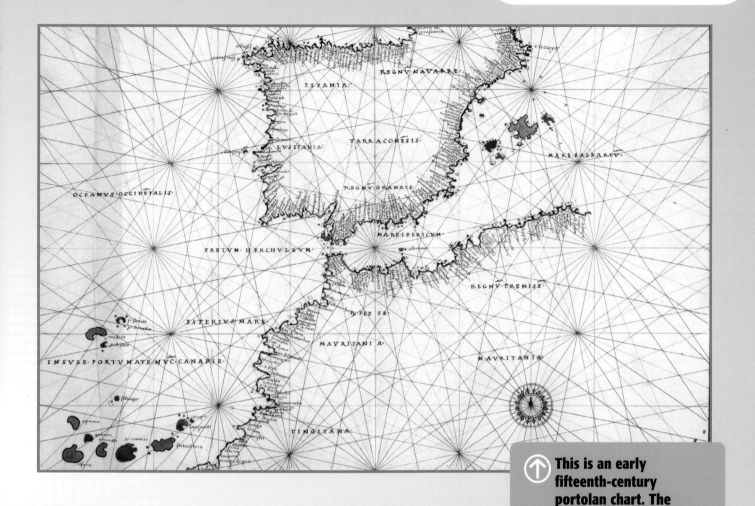

This is an early fifteenth-century portolan chart. The shape of the coastline is complex, and the names of many ports and harbors are supplied.

inland since that had no relevance for sea travelers. Instead, the empty spaces on the charts could be used for the compass roses, scale bars, and written notes about features or hazards.

Chartmakers not only included the names of the main ports and harbors but often added flags and symbols next to important cities. The symbols are useful to modern historians who want to work out who ruled a particular area or city.

As navigational techniques and instruments improved over time, charts became more and more accurate. In the fifteenth and sixteenth centuries, the Portuguese became the main chartmakers as they traveled farther and farther into the Atlantic Ocean. Their country lay on the western edge of Europe, with Spain blocking the way to the east. It was inevitable that the Portuguese would turn their attention to the sea.

While sailors were producing more and more accurate maps of coastlines and sea distances, meanwhile, many land cartographers were still basing much of their work on fantasy, myth, interpretations of the scriptures, and guesswork.

Longitude

As explorers traveled farther away from home, they needed more and more to know their longitude, or how far they had traveled in an easterly or westerly direction.

LINES OF LONGITUDE, CALLED MERIDIANS, ARE imaginary lines on the Earth's surface that run from the North Pole to the South Pole. Longitude is measured eastward and westward from the Prime Meridian (0°), which runs through Greenwich in London, England. The longitude of a point is the angle at the center of the Earth between the meridian on which it lies and the Prime Meridian. The degrees are numbered west and east of Greenwich up to 180°.

John Harrison (1693–1776)

In 1714, the British Board of Longitude announced a competition. Whoever could invent a method for accurately finding a ship's longitude would win a huge prize of £20,000. Being able to work out longitude could give the British huge advantages in international trading and military seapower. It would also help prevent disasters at sea resulting from poor navigation. In order to claim the prize, the winner had to measure a ship's longitude to an accuracy of 0.5 degree, or 30 minutes, of longitude.

People assumed that the prize would go to whoever could devise a way of calculating longitude from astronomical observations. However, clockmaker John Harrison believed that he could win with a very accurate marine clock, or chronometer. His fourth design proved to be accurate enough to win the competition. Tests at sea found that, over a five-month period, it had an error of just 1.25 minutes of longitude, easily accurate enough to win the prize.

➔ Although Harrison's chronometer was accurate enough to win the competition, he had to wait years to receive his prize.

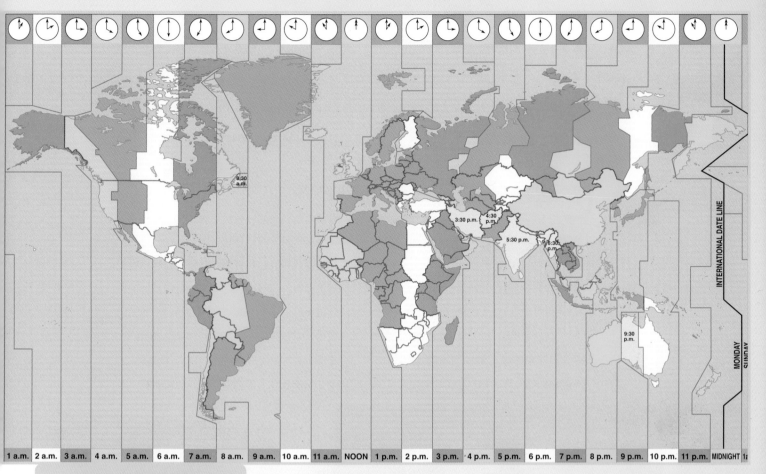

World time zones. The time changes by one hour for every 15° of longitude traveled around Earth. You lose or gain a day crossing the International Date Line.

The Earth turns 360° (a complete revolution) every day and 15° every hour. If a navigator knew the time on the Prime Meridian and also knew the precise local time, it would be simple math to multiply the time difference (in hours) by 15 to give the ship's longitude.

To make this possible, however, sailors needed an accurate way of measuring time. Johan Werner had first suggested using some sort of timekeeper as early as 1514. But clocks were too delicate to keep accurate time in the rough conditions of a sea voyage. Changes in temperature, humidity, and the ship's movement all upset their mechanism. Clocks had to be constantly adjusted. It was not until the eighteenth century that John Harrison's development of the marine chronometer finally allowed navigators to determine their longitude accurately (see box). By referring to nautical almanacs compiled by astronomical observatories, navigators could now work out their position east or west as well as north or south.

23

Captain Cook

Captain James Cook (1728–1779), a British naval officer, made three great voyages of exploration in the Pacific and Atlantic oceans.

COOK'S SKILLS AS A NAVIGATOR AND MAPMAKER WERE exceptional. Cook made his first voyage without a chronometer, so it was difficult to measure longitude exactly. He still managed to accurately map more than 5,500 miles (9,000 km) of newly discovered coastline in the South Pacific. He also carried a group of British astronomers to Tahiti to make observations of the planet Venus. From Tahiti he sailed to New Zealand; he claimed the island for Britain and charted some 2,400 miles (3,900 km) of coastline. In 1770, he charted the east coast of Australia, which he also claimed for Britain and named New South Wales.

The main purpose of Cook's second voyage was to search for a southern continent that many cartographers believed must exist. This time Cook had the new chronometer, which enabled him to calculate his longitude without the need for

← One aim of Cook's second voyage to the Pacific was to search for Terra Australis, the mythical "Southern Continent." This large landmass still appeared on many eighteenth-century maps. Cartographers believed that it must exist near the South Pole in order to balance the large amounts of land that existed in the Northern Hemisphere.

dead reckoning. Cook crossed the Antarctic Circle on January 16, 1773. However, he never reached Antarctica, the southern continent. Cook believed that sea ice continued all the way to the South Pole.

Cook's final voyage began in 1776, when he set sail in search of a Northwest Passage between the Atlantic and Pacific oceans. He reached what is now Oregon and charted the North American coast up to the Bering Strait before being forced to turn south. He decided to resupply and repair his ships in Hawaii, where he was killed by natives in 1779.

James Cook's Diary

These words are taken from Captain James Cook's diary, describing the people of Hawaii (1778). Cook witnessed a traditional pastime still enjoyed by people in Hawaii—and today in many other parts of the world.

"They are open, candid, active people and the most expert swimmers we had met with. The men, sometimes 20 or 30, go without [beyond] the swell of the surf, and lay themselves flat upon an oval piece of plank about their size. They wait the time for the greatest swell and altogether push forward with their arms to keep on its top; it sends them in with a most astonishing velocity. If the swell drives him close to the rocks before he is overtaken by its break, he is much praised."

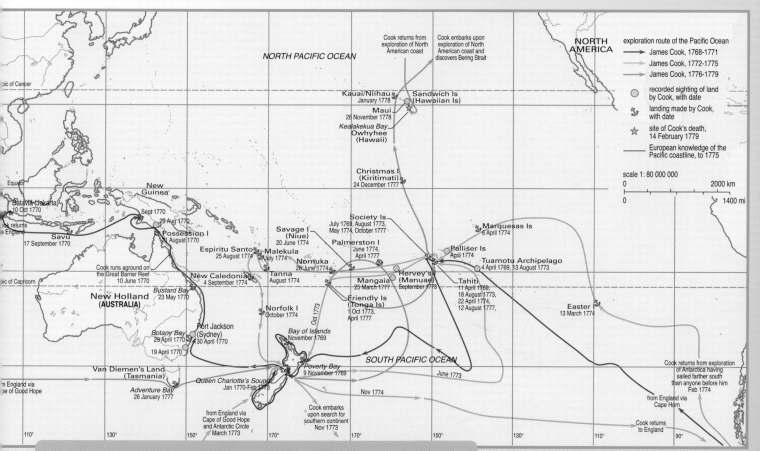

The voyages of Captain Cook in the South Pacific. He was the first European to visit many Pacific Islands and to explore the coasts of eastern Australia and New Zealand. The charts he made were so accurate they were used for many years.

Nautical Charts

As controlling the world's oceans and trading routes became increasingly important to maritime powers, so did the need for accurate nautical charts.

NAUTICAL CHARTS ARE WORKING documents. They are both route maps and work sheets on which the navigator can plot courses and positions. Charts are vital tools for safe navigation, and no ship would venture to sea without all of the charts necessary for the intended voyage.

An extract from a small-scale nautical chart of part of the Caribbean Sea. It shows coastlines, depths, and obstructions such as subsea cables. It is a Mercator projection with a scale of 1:930,000.

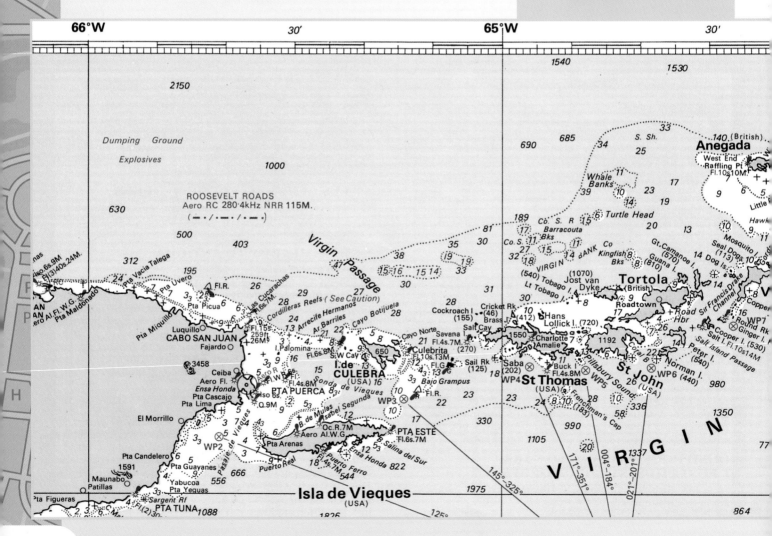

Sea charts have been in existence in a variety of forms, such as portolans, for at least eight centuries. However, official nautical charts date from the development of hydrography (the study of ocean depths and current directions) in the mid-seventeenth century.

Since the 1950s, hydrographers have been able to measure water depth accurately using sonar technology. In previous centuries, however, measuring for maps had had to rely on a lead and line. As its name suggests, this was a lead weight attached to a rope. The rope had depths indicated on it by colored markers. The weight was dropped over the side of the ship, and the marker nearest the water surface showed the depth. Depth was originally measured in units known as fathoms but later in yards or meters.

The length of line and the strength of any tidal currents limited the usefulness of lead and line. The method could only be used close to shore. Measuring accurate depths consistently and in deeper waters had to wait for the development of sonar.

Sonar gets its name from Sound Navigation And Ranging. Sonar uses ultrasonic pulses radiating down from an instrument on the ship and a listening device that receives the pulses reflected from the seabed. The time taken for the pulses to be sent and received allows hydrographers to calculate the depth of the water. Sonar can operate in any depth of water and is not affected by tidal streams or currents.

A Huge Difference in Scales

Hydrographic charts that portray water depths and coastlines are drawn to widely different scales depending on the area covered. A harbor chart has to provide much more information about shipping lanes, jetties, and underwater obstructions than an ocean sailing chart. Hydrographic measurements use the nautical mile, which measures 2,000 yards. (A land mile is 1,760 yards.) Almost all nautical charts use Mercator's projection, where lines of latitude and longitude are at right angles to each other. Although this projection distorts land areas, it provides an accurate representation of bearings (angle of the route away from due north) and angular measurements, so sailors can plot courses and use the bearings to steer their vessel.

Radar

For centuries, navigators relied on paper charts. With the development of small, powerful computers, many charts have been converted to digital form.

CONVENTIONAL PAPER CHARTS HAVE DISADVANTAGES when compared to electronic charts. They are bulky and their storage requires a lot of space on board, especially for a vessel going on a long journey, which must carry all of the charts for that voyage. Using paper charts requires a large chart table that takes up space on or near the ship's bridge. And paper charts need regular updating as hazards or navigational aids such as lighthouses change. Updating charts by hand is time-consuming.

A ship is controlled from the bridge. At night, the bridge operates only with red light; this helps to preserve the crew's night vision for watching for hazards out at sea. To use a paper chart at night, the user must have a light, which risks ruining their ability to see effectively in the dark.

All of the map data of an electronic chart can be stored on a disk or hard drive, and updates can easily be

Ocean-going yachts have a wide range of electronic navigational equipment on board, including radar "globes," seen here on either side of the mast.

downloaded. Electronic charts are also easier to use at night because the display will not harm the user's night vision. Instead of having to unroll a large paper chart, only the relevant area is called up on screen and viewed at any scale. Navigators can zoom in when fine detail is needed or zoom out for a broader picture.

Selecting Information

Showing information digitally on a ship's bridge has a number of other advantages. The detail to be shown can be selected according to the current needs of the vessel. For example, a navigator might want to see the course of a shipping channel but may not need to see the depth soundings. They can easily be left out of the display. The captain of a supertanker with a very deep draught (the depth of the ship below the waterline) can select depths appropriate to the ship, while the navigator of a car ferry with a very shallow draught can select different depth soundings to be displayed for the same area.

Physically changing one paper chart for another is no longer necessary. That reduces any potential confusion in areas of overlap. Sailors can see a large area all at once—which would be awkward using several paper charts at the same time; they can pan across to a new area quite easily. Digital charts also allow the navigator to draw a route diagram onto the chart electronically.

An Unfinished Task

Currently, there is no complete digital coverage of the seas of the world. Not even the International Hydrographic Office has complete paper chart coverage at the largest possible scale. Some government hydrographic offices and commercial companies are in the process of digitally scanning paper charts, but this kind of scanned image is like a digital photocopy and does not have all the advantages of a digital chart.

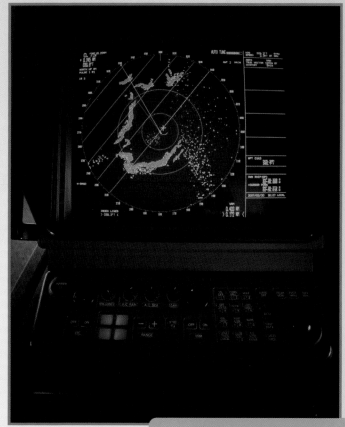

⬆ **Radar display is an instant map. It relies on signals sent out by the ship and bounced back from land and other ships. The screen shows land areas in orange and other vessels as dots.**

An electronic chart is much more than just a digital version of a paper chart. It can be combined with a nautical information system and linked to other shipboard equipment to create an Electronic Chart Display and Information System (ECDIS). This makes marine navigation far more accurate and therefore safer and more economic.

Modern Shipping and ECDIS

Until recent decades, ships carried a wide range of navigational aids, including charts, tide tables, almanacs, and other publications that they relied on to navigate safely. All of these aids come together in the Electronic Chart Display and Information System (ECDIS).

The first two letters of the acronym indicate that part of ECDIS is an electronic chart, with all the advantages that has over the traditional paper chart. It also includes an information system that allows the user to select extra information to be displayed on screen. An example might be a church tower used by navigators as a landmark to fix their position. On a paper chart or a digitally scanned electronic chart, it would be marked with a symbol. ECDIS can give information such as the tower's height and even color. It can also sometimes provide digital images of the tower as seen from the sea.

Bringing Information Together

ECDIS combines the electronic chart system with built-in alarms to warn of possible collisions and groundings, which makes it highly useful to rescue services. ECDIS can be especially helpful in areas where accurate navigation is vital because of the number of possible hazards. Relying on paper charts in busy and complicated shipping lanes can be extremely difficult and potentially disastrous.

ECDIS makes navigating duties easier, faster, and much more precise because it combines different activities. It can be used for route planning; entering observations, instructions, and notes; and working out position.

The core of ECDIS is a powerful computer with a highly precise monitor. It is linked to other items of the ship's equipment such as the gyrocompass, turn indicator, and ship's speedometer. It is also linked to the ship's positioning sensors and in particular to the global positioning system (GPS; see pages 32–35). The GPS can superimpose radar images on top of charts.

Computers Need Input

The quality and amount of information stored is crucial to the success of the system. Some areas of the world have been digitally surveyed, and detailed information is available. For areas surveyed further in the past, paper charts provide the only information. The quality of this information may not be detailed or accurate enough, or at the appropriate scale for ECDIS.

Ships sailing the seas delivering cargoes or passengers are too busy to spend time updating information for ECDIS. So digital scans of paper charts have to be used until there is good world coverage of digital data in a usable format.

ECDIS and radar systems are linked to other items of the ship's navigation equipment. On a modern ship's bridge, the captain has all the information needed.

Global Positioning

The global positioning system, or GPS, is a radio navigation system that relies on satellites placed in space by the U.S. Department of Defense.

IN ANY KIND OF NAVIGATION, FIXING A POSITION requires observations of two or more distant, known locations. They could be landmarks or stars. Positioning from satellites works in just the same way. Two or more satellites provide information that combine to provide a location on Earth. (The system can work using just two satellites, but for accuracy at least three are used.)

The Russian system equivalent to GPS is called GLONASS. It has 21 of these satellites in orbit 11,900 miles (19,100 km) above Earth's surface, each orbit lasting 11 hours 15 minutes.

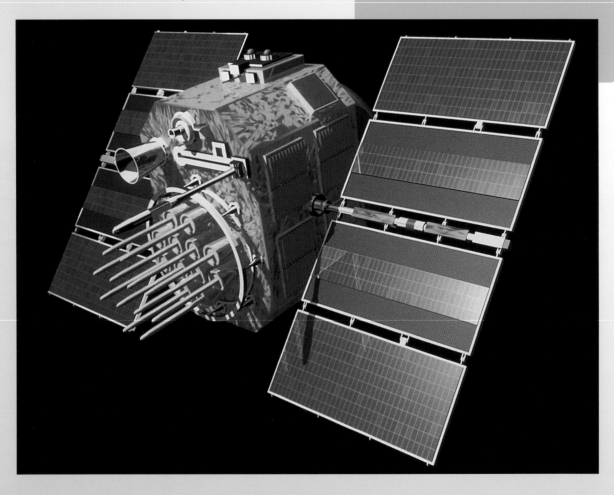

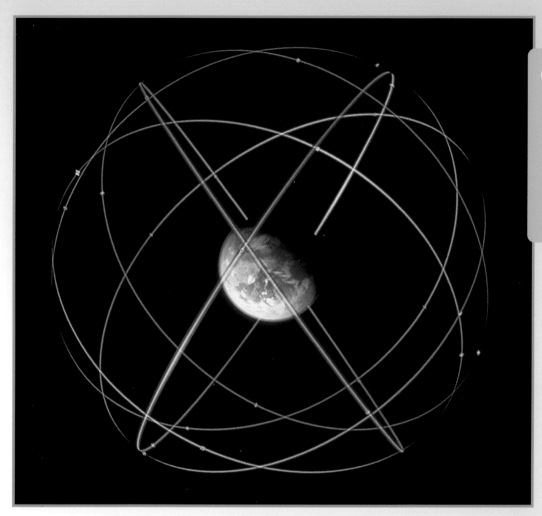

⬅ **With a large number of satellites orbiting Earth, there are always enough to ensure accuracy. Any point on Earth can always receive signals from at least three satellites.**

GPS was developed by the U.S. Department of Defense during the 1970s and 1980s, and became fully operational in 1995. Because the U.S. military set it up and operates it, for years only the military had access to its full capabilities. This restriction was lifted in 2000. Since then, nonmilitary users have also been able to obtain very accurate positions.

There are 24 to 32 satellites, each flying in a circular orbit at an altitude of 10,900 miles (17,540 km) above Earth. They circle Earth every 12 hours. Each satellite has four atomic clocks that provide extremely accurate time. In addition, the position of each satellite is monitored precisely using a system that predicts its orbit. Each satellite broadcasts a unique signal that tells receivers on Earth where the satellite is and what time the signal was sent.

Using its own clock, any receiver on Earth's surface can calculate the time lag between broadcast and receipt of the signal and compute the distance from the satellite. Often, signals from more than three satellites can be sensed. That increases the accuracy of the latitude, longitude, and height position calculation for the receiver.

Three Segments

There are three main parts to GPS: Space, Control, and User segments. The Space segment is the satellites that orbit Earth. Powered by solar cells, they continually adjust their antennae to point toward Earth. The Control segment is the U.S. Air Force base in Colorado Springs and other monitoring stations spread around the world. These stations watch over the satellites and their performance, checking their orbits and making sure that their signals are being properly broadcast.

The User segment is the name given to any military or civilian equipment that receives GPS signals. Such equipment ranges from extremely expensive and sophisticated receivers used by armed forces to inexpensive hand-held sets in civilian use. The large increase in the use of GPS for positioning through phones and in cars means that hundreds of thousands of GPS devices are sold every month.

A hiker checks his position using a small hand-held GPS receiver. In featureless landscapes such as moors or deserts, GPS is invaluable, giving latitude and longitude locations to within 10 to 20 yards.

Not Just for Positioning

Navigation is not the only military use for GPS. It helps military controllers find targets and organize air support. It also guides "smart" weapons—missiles that can lock onto a fixed target. Civilians use GPS for surveying; for air, land, and marine navigation; and to guide emergency services to the scenes of accidents. GPS can even help agriculture by helping measure the size of fields. Without exception, large ships use GPS for navigation.

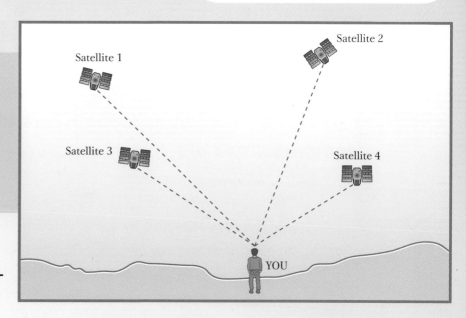

The GPS satellites know their own position and send out a signal with that position and the time of transmission. The receiver on the ground notes the time of arrival of the signal and can figure out precisely how far it traveled.

Even Greater Accuracy

The accuracy of GPS varies. Most hand-held civilian GPS units are accurate to within 10–20 yards in a horizontal position for 95% of the time. The more-complex military devices are more accurate. Neither type of device is as good at calculating height above sea level. A more sophisticated method known as differential GPS can produce an accurate position to within 1 yard. It relies on radio transmission on Earth's surface between a field receiver and a receiver at a known position. Differential GPS can be used on ships close to shore, in shallow waters, or in hazardous areas. The "field receiver" is on board the ship while the receiver is at a known position on the shoreline and broadcasts the corrections needed to the vessel offshore. Surveyors use these radio transmissions to calculate positions to within about one-half inch.

GPS does not rely on good visibility or a stable working platform to operate. With the integration of the technology into mobile phones and in-car navigation systems, GPS has become an important aid to everyday navigation for many people.

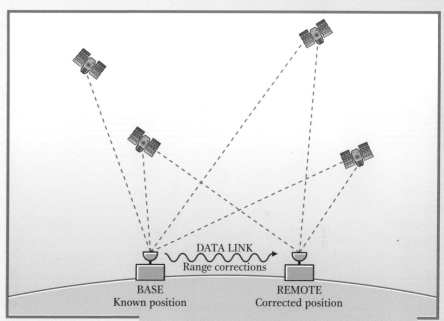

Many possible causes of distortion can reduce the accuracy of a GPS signal. The biggest cause is the atmosphere through which the signal passes. But if there is a local base station at a known position that receives the same signals from at least three satellites, it can figure out what the errors are and supply a radio link correction to the GPS receiver. This is called differential GPS.

Navigating in the Air

Until the 1940s, pilots could only navigate by looking out of the cockpit window, using rivers and mountains as landmarks, and plotting their course on paper maps.

TODAY'S AIRCRAFT FLY MUCH FASTER AND OFTEN AT GREAT altitudes. They also fly above clouds and at night. All flights have to be planned in advance and pilots follow set routes. These routes are designed to be the quickest and therefore the cheapest paths and are usually great circle routes (see box).

Civilian airplanes are controlled by air traffic control systems (ATCS). These systems have three elements: airport towers, terminal radar approach control (TRACON), and en-route centers. The airport towers are responsible for aircraft within about 2 miles (3 km) of the airport. TRACON facilities look after aircraft 2–40 miles (3–65 km) from the airport, using radar to track them. En-route centers monitor and direct

→ To keep in touch with air traffic control systems, aircraft must communicate with the ground, in particular with terminal radar approach control.

Great Circle Routes

You might guess that the shortest distance between two points on a sphere like Earth is a straight line of constant bearing or heading. But it is not. It is in fact a great circle. It lies on a plane that intersects the sphere's—or Earth's—center.

People have known that a great circle route is the shortest distance across the land or the oceans since before the voyages of Christopher Columbus in the fifteenth century. However, sailing ships affected by ocean currents and prevailing winds could not often take advantage of this knowledge.

But aircraft, which can move independently of the wind, use great circle routes because they save time and fuel for all journeys longer than a few hundred miles. To follow a great circle route, the navigator cannot use a fixed compass heading but needs to change heading at regular intervals.

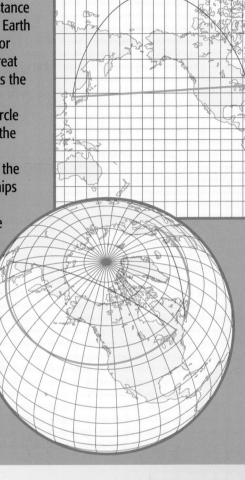

⬆ **On a world map drawn using Mercator's projection, great circle routes are curved lines, shown here in red.**

⬅ **The route seems to make a lot more sense shown on a globe. We are so used to the Mercator projection we forget how much it distorts.**

aircraft after they have reached their cruising altitudes. They also use radar to track the aircraft and human controllers to direct them.

Navigation between airports relies on ground beacons, electronic and computerized equipment on the airplane, and satellite navigation systems. The most widely used ground system is the very high frequency omni-directional range beacon (VOR). These beacons send signals to the aircraft telling the pilot what course to follow and often the distance to or from the beacon. On routes between continents, a system called Omega uses more powerful long-range signals. Onboard computers analyze the signals and calculate the position of the aircraft.

For almost all flights, and certainly for all commercial flights, charts are entirely computer-generated. Images of coastlines and mountain ranges are produced on screen for the pilot. A navigator can guide an airplane around the world without once looking down at Earth's surface.

Changes in the Air

Air navigation relies on radio beacons, radio frequencies, and call signs. A detailed chart is only needed when the airplane is leaving or approaching an airport.

THE VERY FIRST AIRBORNE NAVIGATION AID WAS THE direction-finding (D/F) loop aerial. This aerial coil was rotated by hand until the signal received from a ground radio station was reduced to zero. When no signal was being received, the loop was at 90° to the direction of the ground station. By obtaining D/F bearings on two ground stations in quick succession, and by drawing two lines on a map in the direction of the signals, the navigator could figure out the position of the airplane where the lines crossed.

There were three drawbacks to the D/F system of navigation. First, the airplane had to be in range of at least two ground radio stations. In order to cover the whole of the globe in this way, there would have to

Amelia Earhart (1897–1937)
Amelia Earhart was the first woman to fly solo across the Atlantic, in 1932. In 1935, she flew from Hawaii to California. The distance was even greater than that from the United States to Europe. Several aviators had attempted the trip, but they had all failed—some fatally. There were no ground radio stations in the Atlantic or the Pacific! Like ship navigators centuries earlier, Earhart relied on a compass, a paper map, and dead reckoning. In 1937, she set out to fly around the world with Fred Noonan as her navigator. Their airplane vanished in the central Pacific. Because there was no tracking system, no one will ever know for sure what happened to them.

⊕ **Amelia Earhart and Fred Noonan consult a map of the Pacific showing the route of their last flight.**

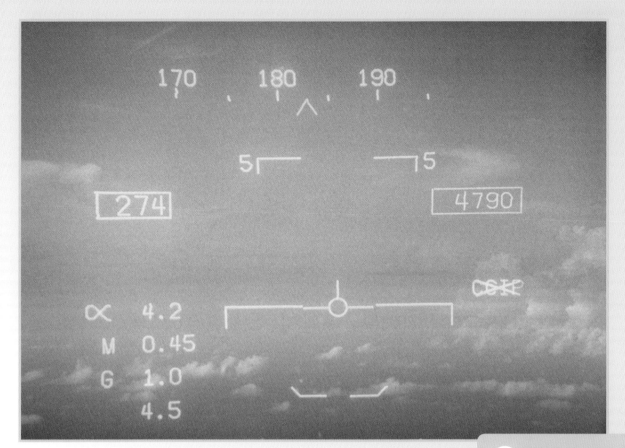

be thousands of stations, which is not practical. Second, the airplane would have to carry a large-scale paper map showing the location of all those stations, which is again impractical on long flights. Third, a route had to fly only from station to station; any deviation meant the airplane risked getting lost.

Despite these drawbacks, this system did not fundamentally change until the introduction of GPS (see pages 32–35). Because GPS information comes from satellites, a pilot does not have to follow routes from ground station to ground station. A navigator can key in a destination and let an automated system decide the best route. A chart is not really needed at all, and traditional navigation skills become less and less important.

Military pilots have very different needs from civilian pilots. Much of their flying is done at low altitudes in order to avoid radar detection, so they are much more likely to need to see where they are going. Because military airplanes are often flown solo and at great speed, there is no opportunity to consult a paper map. Much of the information used by military pilots is projected onto the pilot's visor or cockpit window as a head-up display.

⬆ **HUD information in an F/A-18C Hornet fighter. An essential decision in all mapping becomes a matter of life and death with HUDs: what to leave out! How much information can the pilot absorb at one time?**

Glossary

Words in *italics* have their own entries in the glossary.

altitude – height or vertical distance above mean sea level; or the degrees of *elevation* of a star, the sun, or the moon above the horizon

astrolabe – an early disk-shaped instrument used for measuring the *altitude* of stars above the horizon

Automatic Direction Finder (ADF) – an air *navigation* system that gives an immediate readout of *bearing* to any ground station in range

aviator – somebody who pilots or navigates an airplane

beacon – a navigational aid, such as a lighthouse, that warns or guides ships on their journey

bearing – the direction someone is heading measured as an angle away from north; due north has a bearing of 0 degrees, while due west has a bearing of 270 degrees. Bearing is also sometimes used to describe angular position or direction in relation to any two known points called *waypoints*.

Bering Strait – a narrow body of water connecting the Bering Sea to the Atlantic Ocean, and separating Russia from Alaska

cartography – the skill of making maps; somebody who collects information and produces maps is called a cartographer

celestial globe – a model of the imaginary sphere enclosing the universe, with Earth at the center, that maps the relative position of the planets, stars, and *constellations* as they appear to us in the skies

celestial navigation – navigating by the stars, the sun, or the moon

chart – a map used by sailors to help in *navigation* showing the coasts, rocks, and shallow places of the sea; maps used by airplane pilots are also called charts

chronometer – an accurate clock; usually refers to a marine chronometer used at sea to calculate *longitude*

circumnavigate – to sail all the way around Earth or around a continent or island

compass – an instrument showing the direction of *magnetic north* using a magnetic needle; *bearing* can be calculated by using a compass

The astrolabe was invented in ancient Greece as an astronomical instrument. It was not until the design was refined by Arab scientists that it became a useful and reliable navigational tool.

A pilot calculates his position. Navigation by dead reckoning is still taught to trainee pilots, for use in emergency situations and to check that automatic systems are working correctly.

compass rose – a diagram showing 360 degrees of *bearings*, placed on old maps to help navigators

constellation – a group of stars in the night sky appearing to form a group and normally named with reference to the shape the group takes; for example, the Big Dipper

cross-staff – an instrument used in early *navigation* to determine how far south or north the observer was

dead reckoning – the calculation of the position of a ship or aircraft without observations of the sun, stars, or other heavenly bodies by using a *compass* and studying the record made by the navigator of the ship's course and speed

depth sounding – a measurement of depth recorded on *hydrographic* charts

direction-finding (D/F) loop aerial – an aerial coil that was the first radio *navigation* aid on airplanes. The navigator needed D/F *bearings* on two ground radio stations in quick succession to fix the airplane's position. The successor to the D/F loop was the *Automatic Direction Finder* (ADF).

elevation – angular or vertical distance from Earth's horizon or from sea level to a higher object or point

equator – the line around Earth joining places the same distance from both the North and South *Poles*; it is the line of 0 degrees *latitude*

fathom – traditional unit of measuring water depth at sea, equal to 6 feet (1.85 m)

generation – a period of time between the birth of your parents and your own birth, often taken to be 25–30 years for making calculations about changes in a population

Global Positioning System (GPS) – a system of 24 satellites orbiting Earth and sending out highly accurate radio signals indicating where they are. A GPS receiver held by someone on Earth can interpret the signals and calculate the receiver's position on Earth.

GLONASS – a satellite-based navigation system developed by the USSR, similar to the *Global Positioning System* (GPS)

great circle route – the shortest distance between two points on the *globe*

gyrocompass – a compass that uses a gyroscope instead of a magnetic needle. Driven by a motor, it points to the geographic North *Pole* instead of to *magnetic north* and is not affected by the magnetic fields of nearby objects of iron and steel.

hard drive – the part of a computer that stores large amounts of data internally; information on the hard drive stays even when the computer is switched off

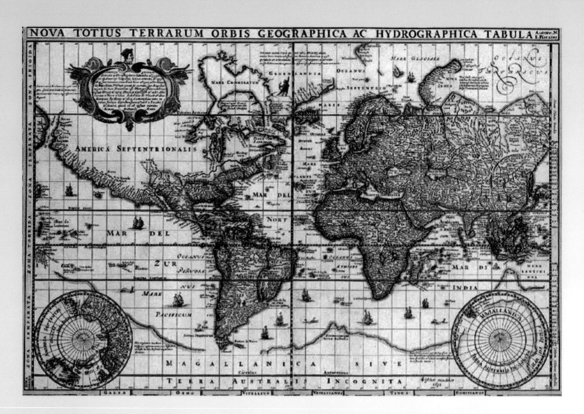

NOVA TOTIUS TERRARUM ORBIS GEOGRAPHICA AC HYDROGRAPHICA TABULA

hemisphere – one-half of the globe. It is divided into northern and southern hemispheres by the *equator* and into western and eastern hemispheres by the *Prime Meridian*.

horizon – the line in the furthest distance where the land or sea and the sky seem to meet

hydrography – the description and study of bodies of water such as seas, lakes, and rivers. Hydrographic charts of oceans and lakes provide navigational information for sailors.

International Date Line – an imaginary line agreed on as the place where each new calendar day begins; it runs from the North *Pole* to the South *Pole* through the Pacific, mostly along the 180-degree *meridian*, but avoiding land

knot – a measurement of speed used at sea; equivalent to 1 *nautical mile* per hour

The Mercator projection was an important advance in the science of cartography. It allowed the curved surface of Earth to be represented as a two-dimensional image without distorting the lines of latitude and longitude. This made it ideal for navigators.

latitude – a line that joins places of equal angular distance from the center of Earth in a north-south direction. The *equator* is at 0 degrees latitude, the *poles* at 90 degrees latitude north and south.

lead and line – a device consisting of a heavy weight and a rope with length markings for measuring depth at sea

lodestone – a hard, black stone (a type of magnetite) that attracts iron and steel as a magnet does, used as an early navigational aid

log – a device consisting of a floating barrel attached to a measured rope for calculating the speed of a ship

longitude – a line connecting places of equal angular distance from the center of Earth, measured in degrees east or west of the *Prime Meridian*, which is at 0 degrees longitude

magnetic north – the northerly direction in Earth's magnetic field, indicated by the direction in which a *compass* needle points

mariner – somebody who pilots or navigates a ship at sea

Mercator projection – a map projection (a method of representing the curved surface of Earth on a flat piece of paper) named after its deviser, Gerardus Mercator (1512–1594), which is commonly used in making nautical *charts*; *bearings* are shown as straight lines on this projection

meridians – lines of *longitude*

monsoon winds – the wind pattern in the northern Indian Ocean, generally from southwest during the summer and northeast during the winter

nautical almanac – a book containing tables giving the position of the stars, sun, moon, and planets for every hour of every day

nautical mile – a measurement of distance used at sea; equivalent to 2,026.7 yards

navigation – plotting a route and directing a ship, airplane, or other vehicle from one place to another; we now use the word to apply to journeys on foot as well

night vision – the ability to see in very low-light conditions as the eyes become accustomed to the dark

padroes – (in Portuguese "padrao"); huge shore beacons first built by the Portuguese probably in the 14th century to help *navigation*

Phoenicians – inhabitants of Phoenicia, an area approximating to modern Lebanon on the eastern Mediterranean coast, who founded a trading empire in the Mediterranean around 3,000 years ago

polar regions – the areas that surround the North and South *Poles*, mainly the Arctic Ocean and Antarctica

poles – the points at either end of Earth's axis of rotation where it meets the earth's surface; the Geographic North and South Poles

Pole Star – sometime called Polaris, it is the closest star in the northern hemisphere night sky to the northern celestial pole; facing it, therefore, indicates that you are facing north

portolan charts – navigational charts used by European sailors from about 1300 to 1600

prevailing wind – the direction a wind blows from most often, exploited by sailing ships for long-distance travel

Prime Meridian – the line of *longitude* at 0 degrees; by international agreement it is the line that passes through Greenwich, London, England

quadrant – an early *navigation* instrument in the shape of a quarter-circle used for measuring the *altitudes* of stars, the sun, the moon, and planets

radar – a method of detecting distant objects by bouncing high-frequency radio waves off them and interpreting the return signal

The Southern Cross constellation is a prominent feature of the flag of New Zealand. A variation on the same design is used on the Australian flag.

raven – a large bird of the crow family with a large beak and black feathers; the *Vikings* used them in *navigation*

rhumb lines – lines of constant *bearing* shown on a chart; on *Mercator projection* they are straight lines, on some projections they curve

sextant – an instrument used by navigators and surveyors for measuring the angular distance between two objects; sextants are used at sea to measure the *altitude* of the sun or a star in order to determine *latitude*

sonar – a device for detecting and locating objects underwater or measuring depth by timing the reflection of sound waves from the sea floor

Southern Cross – a group of four bright stars in the form of a cross, visible in the skies south of the *equator* and used by navigators to locate the direction south

Vikings – warrior seamen and traders from Scandinavia, prominent from the 8th to the 11th centuries

waypoint – a checkpoint on a journey, or a point on a course where a change of *bearing* is needed

wind rose – a diagram showing the direction of *prevailing winds* and placed on *portolan charts* and old maps to help navigators

Further Reading and Web Sites

Aczel, Amir D. *The Riddle of the Compass: The Invention That Changed the World*. New York: Harcourt, 2001.

Arnold, Caroline. *The Geography Book: Activities for Exploring, Mapping, and Enjoying Your World*. New York: Wiley, 2002.

Barber, Peter, and April Carlucci, eds. *The Lie of the Land*. London: British Library Publications, 2001.

Brown, Carron, ed. *The Best-Ever Book of Exploration*. New York: Kingfisher Books, 2002.

Davis, Graham. *Make Your Own Maps*. New York: Sterling, 2008.

Deboo, Ana. *Mapping the Seas and Skies*. Chicago: Heinemann-Raintree, 2007.

Dickinson, Rachel. *Tools of Navigation: A Kid's Guide to the History & Science of Finding Your Way*. White River Junction, VT: Nomad Press, 2005.

Doak, Robin S. *Christopher Columbus: Explorer of the New World*. Minneapolis, MN: Compass Point Books, 2005.

Ehrenberg, Ralph E. *Mapping the World: An Illustrated History of Cartography*. Washington, D.C.: National Geographic, 2005.

Field, Paula, ed. *The Kingfisher Student Atlas of North America*. Boston: Kingfisher, 2005.

Ganeri, Anita, and Andrea Mills. *Atlas of Exploration*. New York: DK Publishing, 2008.

Graham, Alma, ed. *Discovering Maps*. Maplewood, NJ: Hammond World Atlas Corporation, 2004.

Harvey, Miles. *The Island of Lost Maps: A True Story of Cartographic Crime*. New York: Random House, 2000.

Harwood, Jeremy. *To the Ends of the Earth: 100 Maps That Changed the World*. Newton Abbot, United Kingdom: David and Charles, 2006.

Haywood, John. *Atlas of World History*. New York: Barnes and Noble, 1997.

Hazen, Walter A. *Everyday Life: Exploration & Discovery*. Tuscon, AZ: Good Year Books, 2005.

Henzel, Cynthia Kennedy. *Mapping History*. Edina, MN: Abdo Publishing, 2008.

Jacobs, Frank. *Strange Maps: An Atlas of Cartographic Curiosities*. New York: Viking Studio, 2009.

Keay, John. *The Great Arc: The Dramatic Tale of How India Was Mapped and Everest Was Named*. New York: HarperCollins, 2000.

Levy, Janey. *Mapping America's Westward Expansion: Applying Geographic Tools And Interpreting Maps*. New York: Rosen Publishing, 2005.

Levy, Janey. *The Silk Road: Using a Map Scale to Measure Distances*. New York: PowerKids Press, 2005.

McDonnell, Mark D. *Maps on File*. New York: Facts on File, 2007.

McNeese, Tim. *Christopher Columbus and the Discovery of the Americas*. Philadelphia: Chelsea House, 2006.

Mitchell, Robert, and Donald Prickel. *Contemporary's Number Power: Graphs, Tables, Schedules, and Maps*. Lincolnwood, IL: Contemporary Books, 2000.

Oleksy, Walter G. *Mapping the Seas*. New York: Franklin Watts, 2003.

Oleksy, Walter G. *Mapping the Skies*. New York: Franklin Watts, 2003.

Resnick, Abraham. *Maps Tell Stories Too: Geographic Connections to American History*. Bloomington, IN: IUniverse, 2002.

Rirdan, Daniel. *Wide Ranging World Map*. Phoenix, AZ: Exploration, 2002.

Ross, Val. *The Road to There: Mapmakers and Their Stories*. Toronto, Canada: Tundra Books, 2009.

Rumsey, David, and Edith M. Punt. *Cartographica Extraordinaire: The Historical Map Transformed.* Redlands, CA: Esri Press, 2004.

Short, Charles Rennie. *The World through Maps.* Buffalo, NY: Firefly Books, 2003.

Smith, A. G. *Where Am I? The Story of Maps and Navigation.* Toronto, Canada: Fitzhenry and Whiteside, 2001.

Taylor, Barbara. *Looking at Maps.* North Mankato, MN: Franklin Watts, 2007.

Taylor, Barbara. *Maps and Mapping.* New York: Kingfisher, 2002.

Virga, Vincent. *Cartographia: Mapping Civilizations.* London: Little, Brown and Company, 2007.

Wilkinson, Philip. *The World of Exploration.* New York: Kingfisher, 2006.

Wilson, Patrick. *Navigation and Signalling.* Broomall, PA: Mason Crest Publishers, 2002.

Winchester, Simon. *The Map That Changed the World: William Smith and the Birth of Modern Geology.* New York: HarperCollins, 2001.

Zuravicky, Orli. *Map Math: Learning About Latitude and Longitude Using Coordinate Systems.* New York: PowerKids Press, 2005.

Online Resources

www.davidrumsey.com
The David Rumsey map collection. This online library contains around 20,000 historical and modern maps.

http://dma.jrc.it
The mapping collection of the European Commission Joint Research Center. Includes ineractive maps as well as maps documenting environmental and human disasters around the world.

http://etc.usf.edu/Maps/
The University of South Florida's online mapping library. The collection includes historical and modern maps from around the world.

www.lib.utexas.edu/maps
The University of Texas's online map library. The collection includes old CIA maps, historical maps, and thematic maps from around the world.

www2.lib.virginia.edu/exhibits/lewis_clark
An online exhibition at the University of Virginia with information on historic expeditions, including Lewis and Clark.

http://maps.google.com
Google's online mapping resource, includes conventional maps and satellite images for most of the world, as well as street-level photography of Western urban centers.

http://maps.nationalgeographic.com
National Geographic's online mapping service.

http://memory.loc.gov/ammem/gmdhtml/
Map collections from 1500–1999 at the Library of Congress. The collection includes maps made by early explorers, maps of military campaigns, and thematic maps on a variety of topics.

www.nationalatlas.gov
Online national atlas for the United States. Includes customizable topographic maps on a range of different themes.

http://strangemaps.wordpress.com
A frequently updated collection of unusual maps, from maps of imaginary lands to creative ways of displaying data in map form.

www.unc.edu/awmc/mapsforstudents.html
A large collection of free maps, covering many different subjects and regions, hosted by the University of North Carolina.

www.un.org/Depts/Cartographic/
  english/htmain.htm
United Nations mapping agency website. contains maps of the world from 1945 to the present day, including UN maps of conflict areas and disputed territories.

Index

Page numbers written in **boldface** refer to pictures or captions.